PUBLISHED by PARABLES
Earthly Stories with a Heavenly Meaning

PROPHETS:
By
Cynthia Alvarez

PUBLISHED by PARABLES
Earthly Stories with a Heavenly Meaning

Prophets
Cynthia Alvarez

Published By Parables
February, 2019

All Rights Reserved. No part of this book may be reproduced or utilized in any form or by any means, electronic or mechanical, including photocopying, recording, or by any information storage and retrieval system, without permission in writing from the author.

ISBN 978-1-945698-95-8
Printed in the United States of America

Readers should be aware that Internet Web sites offered as citations and/or sources for further information may have been changed or disappeared between the time this was written and the time it is read.

PROPHETS:
BY
CYNTHIA ALVAREZ

PUBLISHED by PARABLES
Earthly Stories with a Heavenly Meaning

CONTENTS

Chapter 1
Who Are Prophets
Page 5

Chapter 2
How Prophets Handle The Word of God
Page 21

Chapter 3
Prophets on the Wall
Page 29

Chapter 4
Gifts
Page 35

Chapter 5
Prophets and the Law
Page 47

Chapter 6
The Dream Team: Prophets and Apostles
Page 59

PREFACE

The Body of Christ is always in a continous state of transition, as God is unapologetically precipitating each consecutive phase of his redemptive plan for mankind. Seeing that each phase is a movement within itself, we understand that prophets will be on the forefront of every phase or movement of God. In fact, God will do nothing in the earth without revealing it to his prophets first. He will reveal it to them first because they are the mouthpiece whereby his purpose and intents are made known in the earthly realm. So, whenever there is a new movement of God, there will be an increase in prophets and false prophets because it is the prophets who promote the purpose of God in the earthly realm, while it is the false prophets who try to derail his purpose. For this reason, God always guarantees that he establishes a sufficient number of qualified prophets for every move he orchestrates as His Kingdom agenda continues to unfold in the earthly realm. And with an ever increasing number of prophets on the scene and still coming on the scene, it is imperative that each one has a thorough understanding of who they are, as well as details concerning their appointed office or calling. This book is written to enlighten and empower the prophets whom God has called forth in this hour. While it does not encompass every aspect of prophets, it will help them to understand who they are, and whose they are. Prophets need to comprehend what God requires of them and what being a prophet means. My goal is to impart wisdom, knowledge, and understanding to everyone who reads this book. I openly declare supernatural increase in every area of your life as you journey to become his prophet, in the phenomenal move of God that is already underway. I pray that you will become abnormally aggressive for the Lord God in this hour, as wisdom is imparted to you throughout this book. Furthermore, I charge you with the responsibility of dispensing the same wisdom to other prophets, who are also in need of the Lord's increase. Eternal blessings to each and everyone of you.

Blessings,
Cynthia Alvarez

Cynthia Alvarez

CHAPTER 1
Who Are Prophets?

Who are prophets? They are God's pivotal Kingdom mouthpieces, gatekeepers, law enforcement officers and warriors. Yes, the duties and functions of a prophet are extensive as should be for such a vital role in the Kingdom of God. Because the charge of the prophet is far reaching and demanding, there is no room for overnight would be prophets in this office. The office or calling of the prophet is not a playground for children nor a daycare for prophetic immaturity by any means. Prophets are not groomed in this office but are groomed before they ever step foot into their role. They must be conditioned beforehand, since being anointed by God and placed in the office of prophet means to be employed by the Almighty God as His Kingdom official. Furthermore, in this office the prophet is ascribed amplified power, authority, and large-scale angelic assistance.

"And he answered, Fear not: for they that be with us are more than they that be with them. And Elisha prayed, and said, LORD, I pray thee, open his eyes, that he may see. And the LORD opened the eyes of the young man; and he saw: and behold, the mountain was full of horses and chariots of fire round about Elisha." (2 Kings 6:16-17)

God would never entrust and endow would be prophets or immature prophets with such weight and endowments when so much is at stake concerning the Kingdom. Relinquishing the reigns of the Kingdom to such unreliable vessels would prove detrimental to the best interest of God's Kingdom. For this reason alone, God is unwavering in his course of action to employ only the best of the best as His Kingdom officials. Nowadays, with such an explosive fascination concerning prophetic activation and operation, there needs to be a more expansive understanding of prophets. People want to hear prophecy and know what tomorrow holds without knowing anything about the nature and role of prophets, who are the mouthpieces that disclose the secrets of God to man. With little understanding of prophets, believers at large have fashioned their own concepts and expectations of what a prophet should be. In most cases, they think a prophet is someone who just sits around and speaks prophetic words every day, as if they are incapable of doing anything more for the Lord or His Kingdom. Yet, many overlook the fact that prophets and apostles are the very officers who established the Kingdom of God on earth. What we have seen in the context of the genuine Kingdom of God on earth in any generation has been a work established by prophets and apostles of God.

"Now therefore ye are no more strangers and foreigners, but fellow citizens with the saints, and of the household of God; And are built upon the foundation of the apostles and prophets,

Jesus Christ himself being the chief corner stone." (Ephesians 2:19-20)

So, if we are to break ground in your understanding of prophets to any extent, we must be able to detail this officer. We must have insight into this officer's **relationship** with God, the structure of the prophet's **anointing**, the **ministry** of the prophet, the **temperament** of the prophet, and the **impact** of the prophet in the Body of Christ to even begin to wrap our minds around this mighty officer of the Lord.

Relationship with God

The unique relationship between God and his prophets is developed in the fiery furnace of afflictions (intense and unpleasant trials/struggles) that they must endure, since this is not a one-dimensional bond. Nor is it a bond confined to or defined by mortality. But it is a relationship that transcends the finitude of the earthly realm to bring the prophets into the very chambers of His eternal realm.

"And the LORD spoke unto Moses face to face, as a man speaks unto his friend. And he turned again into the camp: but his servant Joshua, the son of Nun, a young man, departed not out of the tabernacle." (Exodus 33:11)

God intends for such a relationship to be unbreachable on any level. In fact, He has gone to great lengths in making sure that it has the lowest possible chance of being breached, God allows the fiery furnace of afflictions to produce solidarity of character within his prophets. So, one who is an affirmed prophet of God will possess very dominate characteristics of loyalty, trustworthiness, self-restraint, boldness, and holiness. Such characteristics are pivotal when considering the access prophets have to God, his power, and his eternal realm. The fiery furnace of afflictions that prophets must endure causes them to become completely submissive to God and being coupled with the privilege of having extraordinary access to his realm, prophets are inevitably transformed into staunch defenders of the King and His Kingdom. That's right! When it comes to defending the Kingdom of the Lord God, which includes the King, His Kingdom, His Laws, and His people, prophets are not only loyalist, but they are extremist in the most comprehensive way, as they are devoted to every cause of the King and Kingdom, which means prophets are poised to react on behalf of the Lord Jesus Christ in matters that concern the welfare of the Kingdom. They retaliate against matters that frustrate the stability and advancement of the Kingdom on earth, as they readily engage in confrontational matters that involve the transgression of God's laws. In addition, prophets adamantly safeguard the Body of Christ from the onslaught of God's adversaries., which causes their relationship with him to be at the forefront of all things. Without question, God undoubtedly becomes their number one priority. Since He has made such lavish spiritual investments in his prophets, it is no surprise that he demands nothing less than to be the preeminent influence in their lives. But if this prerequisite is not understood early in the grooming of the prophets, the Lord must take more extensive conditioning measures in the fiery furnace of afflictions to make sure this truth becomes firmly fixated in the minds and hearts of these powerful vessels to derail the possibility of them becoming renegades of the Kingdom. When prophets defect to the position of renegades, they become offenders and nuisances to the King and His Kingdom. Nothing they do as renegades can please God, as they have been disconnected from everything about him that makes them Kingdom officials. So, God is always concerned about establishing a fortified relationship with his prophets, since they are his mouthpiece and defenders of His Kingdom on earth.

Anointing

The anointing of each prophet is tailor-made for the individual assignment that God has appointed them to. Every prophet will not have the same anointing configuration or perform to the same degree because each prophet is spiritually equipped for their assigned post. The caliber of their anointing depends on the people they are assigned to impact, the region they are appointed to, and the spiritual strongholds that they must combat.

"And there arose not a prophet since in Israel like unto Moses, whom the LORD knew face to face, in all the signs and wonders, which the LORD sent him to do in the land of Egypt to Pharaoh, and to all the servants, and to all his land, and in all that

mighty hand, and in all the great terror which Moses shewed in the sight of all Israel." (Deuteronomy 34:10-12)

So, whatever life experiences, talents, outlook, personality traits, belief system, spiritual gifts, angelic assistance, etc., that is necessary for prophets to function as proficient as the Lord would require of them, the prophet's anointing would comprise every attribute that makes it possible for him to meet the Lord's requirements. But the attributes do not all surface at one time. The shaping of a prophet's anointing is progressive because it takes time to dismantle, revamp, and fortify character. Every person is born with biological talents and traits that are as natural in their use as inhaling and exhaling. These traits can be exercised so naturally by the person, until it takes little effort for him to demonstrate the traits and intangible features. As an example, some people have a humorous nature and can take any situation or conversation and fuse it with humor and turn a frown upside down with little to no effort. Others tend to have an innate tendency to take charge in any situation, as leadership just comes natural to them. These are natural traits that can be incorporated into a prophet's anointing to equip them for the vocation of the Lord. Then there are traits that must be cultivated and developed in the prophet's life. Some of these specific traits are diligence, endurance, faithfulness, tenacity, etc. that further enhance the character and anointing of the individual. Yet, these traits do not emerge without the pressure, difficulties, piercing, and burning that must be experienced in the fiery furnace of afflictions. Finally, there is the supernatural aspect of the anointing that prophets receive for the assignment that they are entrusted to fulfill. These include the Spirit of God, spiritual gifts, and angelic assistance, which make up the more impressive components of the prophet's anointing. The greater the assignment committed to a prophet by the Lord, the more substantial the supernatural aspects will be in their life and ministry because God's optimum goal is the success of his servants.

We must fully comprehend that God is the master and chief architect when it comes to crafting the specific power packed anointing of his prophets. It is this anointing that gives them the leverage or advantage needed to accomplish the unshakable will of God. In all honesty, the anointing of mature, equipped, and affirmed prophets should be rich, weighty, and densely layered when compared to an average believers' anointing, which tends to be lighter, more homogenized, and thinly coated. God's reasoning for anointing grade variations among believers within the Body of Christ is simple. He anoints every believer with the capacity to meet the demands of their individual assignment and the wherewithal to overcome the many challenges they will encounter. So, when prophets walk in the fullness of their God ordained anointing, they can effectively engage people, nations, and kingdoms in the capacity that is needed to set the move of God in motion. To be a catalyst for any move of God is an honor that is automatically designated with great responsibility. Being acquainted with weighty responsibility is the reason prophets are not easily overwhelmed by situations that would effortlessly overwhelm the average believer. God conditions them in every necessary way to ensure that his prophets perform precisely as he has outlined for the Kingdom office or role they have been installed into. Nothing less will do.

Ministry

Although powerful in nature and in execution, the ministry of prophets is not always popular among believers. The reason it will not always be well liked is because the ministry of prophets will never involve compromise. They cannot afford to bargain with God's laws. Prophets oversee adherence to these laws in the earthly realm to make certain that God's people are in full alignment to his ordinances. Therefore, prophets have a ministry that opposes, exposes, combats and annihilates actions, lifestyles or systems that execute, promote or indulge in the blatant breaching of his divine laws. For many, it seems as if prophets are harsh, abrasive, heartless, and just plain rude when it comes to addressing the sins and shortcomings in their lives. But the servant of God must attack sin with such ferocity, if he is to expose and root it out of the heart of God's people, as he is fully aware that when sin of any degree goes unchecked, it can become potent enough to cripple local believers and aggressive enough to spread throughout the universal Body of Christ. The crux of a prophet's work can be seen in restraining and eradicating sin from among believers, which is the reason they are not always well received by every person they come in contact with.

"Cry aloud, spare not, lift up thy voice like a trumpet, and shew my people their transgression, and the house of Jacob their sins." (Isaiah 58:1)

For many believers, prophets are bearers of stringent words and forceful decrees that do not excuse or give preferential treatment to their shortcomings. But while it might seem that prophets only spew forth harsh critiques of believers, they are equally engaged in empowering and encouraging those who are in the Body of Christ. The powerful revelations, keen insight, and mighty decrees that prophets exert into the lives of believers are formidable enough to strengthen, stabilize, and energize the minds and hearts of his people. Prophets clearly understand that they are not simply ministering to believers, but they are ministering to God's army of believers, and his army cannot be composed of crippled, downtrodden, and weak prisoners of sin. No, it cannot. But God's army must be composed of righteous, loyal, bold, and unwavering soldiers who have essentially laid down their lives to take up His cause in this earthly realm. Thus, prophets have a major role in making sure that God possesses an army with the quality, stature, and fortitude that he requires for a military that would come to the defense of His Kingdom. After all, God is looking for the best of the best to defend that which is dear to him.

"For many are called, but few are chosen." (Matthew 22:14)

Temperament

Prophets, for the most part, tend to be perceived as weird and almost crazy when viewed under the telescope of the world and even the church world at times. Although they are not crazy, the various aspects of their temperament cause them to be anything but everyday normal people. Prophets have a personality that becomes fused with the Lord's personality to a great degree, which allows these servants to perform precisely as the Lord needs them to. This fusion creates the Lord's outlook within each prophet, so that they will be able to view or perceive matters from God's perspective instead of relying on their humanistic point of view. Such a fusion warrants the coupling of emotions to ensure that prophets are always able to understand the sensitivities of the Lord in relation to His Kingdom, His Laws, His People, and His Adversaries.

"For my thoughts are not your thoughts, neither are your ways my ways, saith the LORD. For as the heavens are higher than the earth, so are my ways higher than your ways, and my thoughts than your thoughts." (Isaiah 55:8-9)

By comprehending the Lord's feelings, prophets will react precisely as the Lord himself would in any given situation to ensure his desired outcome, which is the reason they seem to exhibit extraordinary passion for the Lord. Lastly, having a fusion with the Lord's personality, prophets can often appear to be distracted or mentally preoccupied when in the company of others. It's not that they are intentionally rude or disinterested in others, but that they are consumed by the Lord and his spiritual realm to the extent that they are drawn into his domain by almost the slightest thought. Their interaction with the spiritual realm is constant, so while others might be preoccupied with the everyday activities of life in this earthly sphere, prophets are fully engrossed in the spiritual realm of God. They are inclined to abide where they feel the most at home and experience genuine compatibility, which just happens to be the realm of God. And as always, his goal is to ensure that his servants are successful in assignment and well-rounded in understanding the Person of the Lord God. By knowing the Lord in such a direct and factual way, prophets have the capability of doing more than just scratching the surface of knowledge as it relates to the King and the divine laws that govern His Kingdom. They can accurately detail the very heart of the Lord concerning his laws, while championing his cause through exacting decrees that effectively attack the strongholds of sin in the lives of his people. Prophets cannot help but to respond in such a way to the transgressions of God's law because their temperament has been hot-wired for the Kingdom work that has been set before them to accomplish on his behalf. No genuine prophet of the Lord can sit quietly on the sidelines or stand by idly while the laws of God are blatantly being flouted among believers. Prophets are duty bound, predisposed, peculiarly equipped or anointed, and will not hesitate to defend the Kingdom from the adversaries of their God.

Impact

No other words can be more suitable in describing prophets than 'God's Powerhouse' because of their ability to change the very landscape of this earthly realm by the very words that they speak forth.

"Then the LORD put forth his hand and touched my mouth. And the LORD said unto me, Behold, I have put my words in thy mouth. See, I have this day set thee over the nations and over the kingdoms, to root out, and pull down, and to destroy, and to throw down, to build, and to plant." (Jeremiah 1:9-10)

The words spoken by prophets carry extensive weight and leverage in the spiritual realm of God, which is why God will solidify their character in advance of them being installed into their anointed role or calling as prophet. He must make it clear to these vessels that the power that is working in and through them to accomplish mighty works belongs to him alone, so apart from him they can do nothing to enhance the Kingdom. Once this is firmly etched in the heart of prophets, God can release greater measures of his extraordinary power through their lives for the benefit of impacting others. Not only are prophets to receive this greater measure of power flowing in and through them, but they must understand how this power is working in their lives as well. Being a prophet of God means that the source of your spiritual power and insight comes from the Lord God. It is important that prophets understand this, since false prophets have a source of spiritual power too, which comes from demons and fallen angels in the Kingdom of Darkness. Although the Kingdom of God and the Kingdom of Darkness are both in the spiritual realm, they operate on different spiritual networks. So, it is important for prophets to be thoroughly groomed to know the difference. Being locked into the spiritual network of the Kingdom of Darkness is to be disconnected from the richness of God's spiritual flow. Unfortunately, this is where many immature or would be prophets find themselves when they are gift-led and not Christ groomed. It is also the place where prophets who have been rebellious and disobedient to the Lord God find themselves after they have been banned from connecting to the Lord's spiritual network. They will try to regain access to the spiritual realm by means of any network they can tap into at this point and become renegades of the Kingdom of God. Operating from the spiritual network of the Kingdom of Darkness causes their work to be contaminated and unfit to effectively equip the Body of Christ for the hour at hand. Moreover, when the Body of Christ becomes more enamored by the gifts of prophets than the sanctity of prophets, deception is inevitable. People who are gift-led simply want to receive insight, information, and answers from the spiritual realm with little concern for the prophets' spiritual affiliation. They will sit at anyone's spiritual table and feast off every word they hear because they are unskilled in knowing the difference between those prophets who are members of God's workforce and those prophets who are employees of the Kingdom of Darkness. Therefore, believers must exercise extreme caution when seeking spiritual information and insight from those who boast in having the title of prophet, yet they clearly lack the character of God on many levels. Having the ability to retrieve information from the spiritual realm does not validate anyone as a prophet of the Lord God, nor does it mean you are tapped into his spiritual flow. There is a lot of information in the spiritual realm that is considered public records and any spiritual being can access the data. In this aspect, it is equivalent to the physical realm we live in because anyone can access vital information that is considered public records. But just as public records in the physical realm consists of former or older information about a person, public records in the spiritual realm consist of previous data about the people. You must understand that spiritual information does not die. It continues to exist because whether it is old or new information that came from God, it is alive, powerful, and sharp. For this reason, the enemy has been successful in leading people into captivity, but believers who are truly locked into God's spiritual flow will always be ahead of the enemy who uses outdated information from previous moves of God to deceive the unenlightened. Again, the enemy depends on public records in the spiritual realm to lure weak believers into the grips of his stronghold of deception. Yet, prophets and apostles will always be on the cutting edge, since they are the Kingdom officials who receive the fresh manna or firsthand revelations from God. Clearly, these mighty officers know their God and they are specialists when it comes to exercising the powers of the world to come. First and foremost, prophets must be sure that it is the power of God working in their lives and not another power.

"Beware of false prophets, which come to you in sheep's clothing, but inwardly they are ravening wolves. Ye shall know them by their fruits. Do men gather grapes of thorns, or figs of thistles? Even so every good tree bringeth forth good fruit; but a corrupt tree bringeth forth evil fruit. A good tree cannot bring forth evil fruit, neither can a corrupt tree bring forth good fruit. Every tree that bringeth not forth good fruit is hewn down and cast into the fire. Wherefore by their fruit ye shall know them. Not everyone that saith unto me, Lord, Lord, shall enter into the kingdom of heaven; but he that doeth the will of my Father which is in heaven. Many will say to me in that day, Lord, Lord, have we not prophesied in thy name? and in thy name have cast out devils? and in thy name done many wonderful works? And then will I profess unto them, I never knew you; depart form me, ye that work iniquity." (Matthew 7:15-23)

The only way they can be sure of this is to solidify their relationship with the Lord God through loyalty, obedience, and holiness. Without these essential qualities being established in them, God could never entrust such power to anyone, seeing that the impact they might have in the lives of others could prove detrimental. The importance of having these essential characteristics and being connected to the correct spiritual network is to make sure that God's spiritual flow is not impeded in anyway as it flows through the prophet, who will release this power into the lives of others. The difference between the spiritual flow of God through a prophet and the spiritual flow from the Kingdom of Darkness is not only seen by what is released into the lives of others, but the effect it has on the prophet himself. The spiritual flow of God builds, enhances, and upgrades the prophet. Yet, the spiritual flow from the Kingdom of Darkness does just the opposite by distorting, contaminating, and downgrading the prophet. Secondly, prophets must know how to handle the word of God that they have been entrusted with. Simply speaking forth a word immediately because it flowed from God does not constitute properly handling the word of God. More is involved than just speaking forth a word. For prophets, **timing**, **precision**, **delivery**, and **purity** are key factors in handling the revealed word of God. The combined execution of these factors will ensure that the word of God is released with the most potent capabilities and in the most effective manner as any mature prophet of the Lord God knows quite well.

CHAPTER 2
How Prophets Handle the Word of God

In chapter one, we discussed the subject of prophets and who they are as it relates to their relationship with the Almighty God. Yet, nothing is more captivating than being an eyewitness to a prophet handling or managing the revealed word of God. Seeing that the word comes directly from God makes it obvious that the prophet is handling more than just words. In fact, he is managing and distributing God's power because the word is dynamic.

Timing
Of all that a prophet receives and gathers from God and His spiritual realm, timing is of the utmost important, since it is the catalyst for executing the word of God. Yes, precision, delivery, and purity have vital roles in handling God's word, but without these internal factors being utilized at the appropriate moment in time, that word will not be able to function in the capacity necessary to effectively impact a person or situation. Timing links these internal factors with specific external factors to solidify success in handling the revealed word of God. The external factors would be the person or people the prophet is sent to, the place or location where the prophet must deliver the word of God, and the unseen angelic assistance necessary to perform that word. So, without the word being delivered at the appropriate time, the

person or people that need to hear it might not be at the designated place or location for the prophet to deliver the word. If the deliverance of the word is not done at the appointed time of God, the prophet is not in sync with God. And if this happens, the angels cannot take the necessary action to accomplish that word because without the coupling of the internal and external factors, they are restrained from engaging in the situation.

"To everything there is a season, and a time to every purpose under the heaven." (Ecclesiastes 3:1)

Angels move and perform in excellence as God's mighty Kingdom liaisons, which means that if the prophet is not in sync with God's timing, the angels would not be able to undergird or support that word, since it would prevent them from performing in perfect alignment with God. Therefore, prophets must be keen in understanding the accuracy of time when releasing the revealed word of God.

Precision

The prophet must be a vessel of precision when handling the word of God, as he is the mouthpiece of the Lord. Not only must he be a vessel of precision, but a vessel of honor and integrity as well, seeing that God is entrusting him with the powers of the Kingdom. The ministry work of the prophet is very demonstrative within itself, and there is no room for error since lives can be both voluntarily and involuntarily impacted by it. Voluntary impacting can be seen when individuals seek out a prophet for truth and insight concerning specific situations in their lives. Involuntary impacting can be seen when God sends the prophet to individuals, at his discretion, to warn, expose, or bring judgment against their sins. In any case, the prophet must be sure of what he is speaking forth and must be skilled in knowing the differences between the voice of God, the voice of his own mind, and the voice of the enemy. If there is any measure of uncertainty in this area of skill, the prophet runs the risk of speaking a contaminated word that could cause much damage in the lives of those he ministers to. Nothing discredits the King and His Kingdom more than an unreliable prophet who has no desire to hone his prophetic gifts. It is the responsibility of the prophet to hone or sharpen his prophetic skills. It is the responsibility of the prophet to walk in holiness before the Lord God. By doing these things, he becomes more useful to the Lord, which should be the goal of all prophets.

"Wherefore the rather, brethren, give diligence to make your calling and election sure: for if ye do these things, ye shall never fall." (2 Peter 1:10)

If you are professing to be a prophet, but seldomly called upon by the Lord for his countless assignments of impacting lives in the earthly realm, something is wrong. There is obviously something lacking in your prophetic skillset or your level of sanctification before God that would disqualify you from abundant opportunities of usefulness to the Lord. Make no mistake about it, the Lord delights in using his qualified human vessels for an undetermined length of time. So, when a prophet makes himself useful and valuable to the Kingdom, the Lord will surely call upon him for service time and time again because he employs only the best of the best in His Mighty Kingdom.

Delivery

Delivering the revealed word of God is crucial because it determines the condition of that word when released into the lives of others. Therefore, prophets must understand the more intricate details in properly delivering or transporting God's word. Every prophet must realize that when God releases a word into their spirit, the word is pure, complete, and in its most powerful form to accomplish the ultimate will of God. The responsibility of the prophet at this point is to keep that word intact until it is delivered to the intended recipient(s), which means he is not to affix anything to it or delete anything from it, as the word must remain as solid as when he first received it from the Lord God.

"For thou shalt go to all that I shall send thee, and whatsoever I command thee thou shalt speak." (Jeremiah 1:7)

The word must be safeguarded from everything within the prophet that could pose a threat to its effectiveness. Knowing that the flesh nature within all humanity opposes everything about God and His Kingdom, very stringent measures had to be put in place to overpower this internal enemy, if the prophet is to be successful in delivering the word of God. When the Lord grooms a prophet, it is done with the objective being to establish a reliable and holy vessel who is capable of functioning as his irrefutable mouthpiece. To achieve this goal, the Lord must overpower the flesh nature within the vessel. Every aspect of the flesh nature (mind, will, and emotions) must be dealt a decisive blow through strategically intensified trials and struggles, which prove to be overwhelming enough to force the flesh nature into an inoperable position. Once the flesh nature becomes inoperable, the word of God has a clear passage way to move through the prophet's being, without interference. If the Lord does not deal with the flesh nature in such a way, the human mind of the prophet would dissect the word of God and interpret it through his own point of view. The will of the prophet would respond to the word in his own best interest and the prophet's emotions would either cause him to move ahead of God's will or avoid his will all together. By the time the flesh nature is done processing the word of God, it is no longer pure, complete, and potent, but becomes diluted and cannot perform to God's standard of excellence. Every prophet has the important responsibility of overpowering their flesh nature from day to day, if they desire to be useful to the Lord. The goal is for the word to be successfully released into the lives of others and be impactful to the highest degree, which requires it being identified with its source. Without mistake, that source is the Lord God. This means that the word must be released in a manner that will keep it fully identified with the Lord. For ex: ("Thus says the Lord God...") or

("The Lord is saying to you...") or ("Surely the Lord says...") or "The Spirit of the Living God is saying...").

"Moreover, the word of the LORD came to me, saying, Go and cry in the ears of Jerusalem, saying, thus saith the LORD; I remember thee, kindness of thy youth, the love of thine espousals, when thou went after me in the wilderness, in a land that was not sown. Israel was holiness unto the LORD, and the first fruit of his increase: all that devour him shall offend; evil shall come upon them, saith the LORD." (Jeremiah 2:1-3)

Prophets should be diligent in keeping the revealed word identified with its source because the work of false prophets and Satan is to keep the revealed word from being identified with God. Such actions will promote a hunger in being gift-led instead of God led. Furthermore, referencing scripture when releasing a word further substantiates the word in the heart of the recipient. Remember, effectiveness is the prophet's goal. When the word of God is delivered properly and consistently by the prophet, he will eventually be considered a loyal vessel who is able to be entrusted with greater matters of the Kingdom.

Purity

The caliber of work performed by the prophet in releasing the word of God can only be measured in its purity, as contamination in any form would cause it to cease from being a divine work. The supernatural aspect from God's divine realm would not be involved in the performance of that word, since purity is the platform that gives way to the manifestation of his superlative power. The mighty angelic force that executes the word of a prophet will only exert power and influence when the prophet creates an atmosphere that reflects the divine realm of God through purity, since they operate in the excellence of his divine will. The prophet must present proper grounds through which the angelic force of God can operate from. Purity is that ground that allows for such action to be taken. If purity is absent, the work of the prophet becomes a work of human effort or even demonic intervention and God is never glorified in situations that promote impurity as the means to accomplishing what he no longer endorses. In some instances, a prophet can be found unfit for further use by the Lord because of the absence of purity. When the Lord determines such a one to be inadequate for impending Kingdom work, he will replace them with a more suitable prophet.

"And the LORD said to Samuel, Behold, I will do a thing in Israel, at which both the ears of everyone that heareth it shall tingle. In that day I will perform against Eli all things which I have spoken concerning his house: when I begin, I will also make an end. For I have told him that I will judge his house forever for the iniquity which he knows; because his sons made themselves vile, and he restrained them not." (I Samuel 3:11-13)

For this reason, the servants of God must be firmly rooted in purity, if they are to join forces with God's mighty angels and impact this earthly realm in the capacity that satisfies His Kingdom purpose. It is impossible for any prophet to accomplish the will of God without an angelic force backing him, so it behooves this servant of God to make purity his priority.

CHAPTER 3
Prophets on The Wall

In the previous chapter we explored how prophets handle the word of God, which is a necessary component of their official duties. Yet, an equally vital aspect of the prophets' official duties is securing the Kingdom. Nothing is more essential to the national security and longevity of any nation, kingdom or country than having a fully functioning defensive system and highly advanced intelligence agency. The Kingdom that God is establishing on earth is not without these same pressing needs. Therefore, it is understood that the citizens of His Kingdom must be thoroughly protected, and governing officials need to have unobscured insight into the objectives of their evil spiritual counterparts. Not only must they have insight into these matters, but they must also stay in constant communication with their commander-in-chief, Jesus Christ, to stay abreast of all new developments pertaining to the Kingdom.

"*I have set watchmen upon thy walls, O Jerusalem, [which] shall never hold their peace day nor night: ye that make mention of the LORD, keep not silence.*" (Isaiah 62:6)

"*But if the watchman sees the sword come, and blow not the trumpet, and the people be not warned; if the sword come, and take [any] person from among them, he is taken away in his iniquity; but his blood will I require at the watchman's hand."* (Ezekiel 33:6)

By now, it should be clear that the work of prophets moves along these lines, and as they function accordingly, these officers become watchmen on the wall or watchmen on the perimeters of the Kingdom of God. When prophets are on the wall, they fortify or strengthen the Kingdom of God on earth. How do they strengthen the Kingdom of God on earth? They secure the perimeters of the Kingdom by patrolling the spiritual realm to prevent the enemies of God from breaching the borders of the Kingdom. Prophets will be the first to identify impending threats to the Kingdom and sound the alarm to warn the people of God, so they can prepare for what is approaching. It does not take a rocket scientist to see that it is impossible for them to secure the Kingdom without being on the wall or in the spiritual heights of God. If their designated place is on the wall, prophets have no time to be distracted by or solely devoted to nurturing a civilian lifestyle for themselves. In other words, they cannot view themselves as everyday civilians who are concerned with popularity, amassing material possessions, being involved with every social event taking place, attached to every trend that keeps the world mesmerized, etc. They simply do not have time for fundamental things of that nature. Please do not misinterpret what is being said here. I am not saying that prophets must be unpopular, poor, excluded from social events or not aware of what is trending in the world. I am saying that none of these things will be of greater concern for them than securing the Kingdom of God and exposing the schemes of God's enemies, which happens to be a full-time occupation that consumes every area of their lives. They are simply not preoccupied with being part and parcel to this world system in any measure. The bible is filled with prime examples of prophets who understood that they could no longer be among the civilian population when they were called by God to take their place on the wall for the work of the Kingdom. Moses left the luxury of being part of the royal family of Egypt to enter the service of God by taking up his mantle and rising to the occasion of securing the Kingdom of God. John the Baptist could be found in the wilderness wearing animal skins and executing the work of the Kingdom, rather than being in the comfy confines of the city with the general population. Jesus left the glory of heaven to take on flesh, so that he could carry out the will of His Father in this earthly realm. Each was a servant of God and they understood the importance of being on the wall as Prophets.

Moses

"By faith Moses, when he was come to years, refused to be called the son of Pharaoh's daughter; Choosing rather to suffer affliction with the people of God, than to enjoy the pleasures of sin for a season; Esteeming the reproach of Christ greater riches than

the treasures in Egypt: for he had respect unto the recompence of the reward. By faith he forsook Egypt, not fearing the wrath of the king: for he endured, as seeing him who is invisible." (Hebrews 11:24-27)

John the Baptist

"In those days came John the Baptist, preaching in the wilderness of Judaea, and saying, Repent ye: for the kingdom of heaven is at hand. For this is he that was spoken of by the prophet Esaias, saying, the voice of one crying in the wilderness, prepare ye the way of the Lord, make his paths straight. And the same John had his raiment of camel's hair, and a leathern girdle about his loins; and his meat was locusts and wild honey. Then went out to him Jerusalem, and all Judaea, and all the region round about Jordan." (Matthew 3:1-5)

Jesus

"Let this mind be in you, which was also in Christ Jesus: Who, being in the form of God, thought it not robbery to be equal with God: But made himself of no reputation, and took upon him the form of a servant, and was made in the likeness of men: And being found in fashion as a man, he humbled himself, and became obedient unto death, even the death of the cross." (Philippians 2:5-8)

The entirety of their life's work was securing the Kingdom through strict obedience to God. When prophets are taken out of the general population to enter the service of the Lord, many things that they once possessed will be lost for the Kingdom's sake. Bills will get behind, relationships will be severed, houses will be foreclosed on, cars will be repossessed, health issues will arise, and so on. It comes with the territory, but if they are on the wall and focused on the work that has been set before them, nothing lost for the cause of the Kingdom will pull them off the wall or from God's service, since they are fully aware of the cost of being his prophet. God makes sure his prophets clearly understand that whatever they lose for the sake of the Kingdom will be restored to them a hundred times over.

"And everyone that hath forsaken houses, or brethren, or sisters, or father, or mother, or wife, or children, or lands, for my name's sake, shall receive a hundredfold, and shall inherit everlasting life." (Matthew 19:29)

Although prophets will possess an undeniable depth of boldness as it relates to protecting the Kingdom, it should never be confused with arrogance in anyway. An arrogant or prideful prophet could never properly secure the Kingdom, since he would constantly need the validation of people to caress his ego. His focus would be fixated on the realm of civilian life. As a result, the borders of the Kingdom would be loosely protected. Yet, when prophets are on the wall, they are strategically positioned by God for the fortification of the Kingdom. Seeing themselves as civilians on any level is a misapprehension all together. They are officials of the Kingdom and for them, civilian life is simply not in view when it comes to being positioned on the wall. It must be this way because God needs His prophets to be effective to the highest degree. He needs their full attention, so that when He is ready to divulge the next phase of his plans, the prophets are spiritually positioned to receive it and poised to declare it to the Body of Christ. In addition, they must be fully alert in the spiritual realm to properly secure the borders of the Kingdom, since they frequently engage in warfare at a moment's notice.

CHAPTER 4
Gifts

In chapter three, we dealt with the importance of prophets being on the wall of the Kingdom, since they are the defensive system that God has set in place to fortify his earthly domain. Yet, being on the wall requires one to be skillful and vigilant to the highest degree. A prophet will never be taken seriously by anyone when he is unskilled in the use of his spiritual gifts. It is the responsibility of this servant to hone and master the spiritual gifts that have been imparted to him, if he truly desires to become more than just a run of the mill Christian. He must know his gifts and understand the usefulness of each. He must know which gifts are more dominant than others in his ministry and the reason for them being more paramount. In doing so, he will be capable of ministering more effectively, as he comes against the spiritual strongholds of sin in the lives of believers and their defection from worshipping God to serving other lesser gods. In addition, prophets must understand that warfare comes with the territory of their duties because operating in spiritual gifts involves handling revelation. Why does revelation produce warfare for prophets? Well, it creates warfare for them because revelation enlightens, empowers, enriches, edifies, directs, and shifts those who receive it. Revelation works for the overall betterment of the people of God, which is the primary reason Satan not only declares war against prophets who release revelation, but he viciously assaults believers who receive revelation of any degree. It does not take a genius to see that if revelation works for the overall betterment of the people of God, it must function in detriment to Satan and his Kingdom of Darkness. As soon as revelation is released from the mouth of the prophets into the lives of believers, Satan wages strategic and intense warfare against them in efforts to prevent the manifestation of the revelation in the lives of the believers. This enemy will throw everything he has at them, including the kitchen sink because he fights viciously, hits below the belt, and has no intentions of fighting fair. Prophets must be skillful warriors and they must be able to prepare the Body of Christ to engage in effective warfare, since confrontation with the enemies of God is inevitable. These mighty officers must be well versed in the knowledge and operation of spiritual gifts. Prophets must master gifts that have not even begun to surface in the lives of many people whom they are called to minister to. The more exceptional prophets become in executing their gifts, the much more helpful or useful they are to God and His Kingdom.

Let's take a quick glance at some of the spiritual gifts that prophets operate in as they minister to others.

Word of Knowledge

If a prophet is to be effective in coming against strongholds, he will do so by operating in the appropriate gifts while ministering, which would start with the word of knowledge, since it gives him the ability to identify or expose the root cause of spiritual strongholds. When operating in this revelatory gift, a prophet has the capability of gaining information or facts about a person's background, lineage and present life condition, which under any other circumstance would be impossible to ascertain. Such information is garnered from an individual's historical record of life that exists in the spiritual realm and must be retrieved through the utilization of spiritual faculties. Jesus demonstrated the operation of this gift when he spoke to the woman at the well.

"Jesus saith unto her, Go, call thy husband, and come hither. The woman answered and said, I have no husband. Jesus saith unto her, thou hast well said, I have no husband: For thou hast had five husbands; and he whom thou now hast is not thy husband; in that sadist thou truly. The woman saith unto him, Sir, I perceive that thou art a prophet." (John 4:16-19)

If a prophet is to contend with spiritual strongholds in the lives of people, he will have to become skillful and comfortable with operating in the word of knowledge, since he must be able to expose the sin or root cause of their bondage. When operating in this gift, the goal is to liberate a person by illuminating their heart and mind with truth. This truth will bring clarity in how the individual came into spiritual bondage and reveal what it takes for them to be emancipated from the stronghold all together. Furthermore, a skillful prophet will not fail to follow up the word of knowledge with the word of wisdom, as his desire is to not only see people free from bondage, but to see people successful at living free.

Word of Wisdom

The word of wisdom is a powerful gift of revelation that is instrumental in prompting movement within the life of an individual. It is also a gift that many people tend to confuse with the gift of prophecy, since both gifts disclose future truths. Yet, the most striking difference between these gifts is seen in how the disclosed truth is fulfilled within the person's life. Through utilization of the word of wisdom, a prophet acquires information or facts about subsequent and future aspects of the individual's life that is used to place the person on course with God's purpose for his life. Instead of wandering around aimlessly with little to no idea of what the future holds for him, the word of wisdom gives the individual a peak into his future. In fact, it points him in the right direction for progress in God. But the word of wisdom only provides insight to an aspect of God's will for an individual's future or next step. It is the responsibility of the individual to work together with God through faith and obedience in the fulfilment of the word of wisdom. For practical reasons, it might be more suitable to style this working relationship as a joint venture involving two parties who are both responsible for certain aspects in the manifestation of a revealed word. God divulges the word of wisdom to the individual by his prophet to produce hope and induce movement in his life. Then the individual must move in faith that is coupled with works to achieve the specific outcome that was detailed in the word of wisdom. Without receiving the word of wisdom, there is no direction for the individual to follow or divine outcome of achievement. Unfortunately, the individual's life will abide in a place of stagnation, unless the word of wisdom is delivered to them. Clearly, there is never any glory in being stagnant, hopeless or falling short of reaching destiny. The word of wisdom is a gift that is indeed powerful enough to change lives, it only needs to be released in accordance to his will.

Prophecy

Prophecy is solely about God disclosing his sovereign will, its effects on and dealings with humanity as well as the rest of creation. He will always make his will or actions known concerning this earthly realm before ever lifting a finger to execute it. Why? God does so to make it perfectly clear that the performance, demonstration, and power that is about to be exhibited is strictly his work. Therefore, God uses prophets as spokesmen, mouthpieces, and promoters who speak forth his purpose and intents in the earth.

"Behold, I will do a new thing; now it shall spring forth; shall ye not know it? I will even make a way in the wilderness, and rivers in the desert. The beast of the field shall honor me, the dragons and the owls: because I give waters in the wilderness, and rivers in the desert, to give drink to my people, my

chosen. This people have I formed for myself; they shall shew forth my praise." (Isaiah 43: 19-21)

God will not allow anyone else to take the credit for what only he can do, so he sends forth prophecy to be announced, declared, publicized, broadcasted or heralded as a precursor of his actions. God wants the inhabitants of the earth and even the onlookers in the spiritual realm to see or witness what he is doing. One of the reasons he utilizes prophecy is to get the attention of whoever he is formally addressing and stimulate a particular response from them. Other reasons God uses prophecy is for warning, judgment, encouragement, promotion, and edification. These each produce the outcome or impact that God purposes for humanity and creation at a given time. Whether the course of an individual's life is changed, a nation is transformed, or the global earth itself is refined, prophecy is the vehicle that causes it to transpire.

Discernment

The gift of discernment is necessary for prophets of any capacity to operate in, since it helps to identify intruders and threats to the Kingdom of God that cannot be easily identified by our natural faculties. Discernment functions similarly to our immune system, which we do not see, but we know it is part of our internal composition because of how it responds to bodily threats from foreign matters. Think about it, most of us do not realize that we have contracted a bacterial infection until we are running a high fever and having difficulty swallowing because of swollen glands caused by strep throat. At this point, we must take proper actions to rid ourselves of this health issue. Making a visit to the doctor and receiving a prescription for antibiotics is the most effective solution when the medication is taken as instructed. Once the antibiotics rid the body of the foreign bacteria that spawned the infection, the immune system can return to its normal, healthy, and unbothered state. Well, that is a similar pattern to how the gift of discernment functions. As prophets, we interact with people on a day to day basis, and with our natural senses or faculties, we only see the outer person. In fact, we have no way of knowing who or what spiritual entity might be influencing them unless we are operating in the gift of discernment. If we are operating in discernment, something inside of us will go off like an alarm to alert us of a possible threat. It will make us aware of a spiritual presence being in close-proximity to us that is evil in nature. Usually, your body will respond in some noticeable manner because of the foreign or evil spiritual presence. The hairs on your body might stand on end, while your insides seem to be twisted in knots. You might incur a bitter taste in your mouth as well, yet how you respond to this ungodly spiritual entity depends on the circumstances. If it is someone who desires deliverance, stand in the authority of the Spirit of God by using the word of God coupled with the power of the blood of Jesus. Do not relent until that ungodly stronghold of demonic influence is dismantled and removed. Once the captive is set free, they need to receive the baptism of the Holy Spirit, so they can live a victorious life in Christ. However, if you encounter a demonic stronghold or influence and the person makes is known that they are not seeking deliverance, leave them be and move on to greener pastures so to speak. The important thing is that you were able to identify the spiritual threat or intruder. When you identify or expose a demonic stronghold or influence, you deal a powerful blow to the Kingdom of Darkness, since the strength of the enemy is in them not being detected. Just to give you a snippet of spiritual insight, a demon that is exposed by the power of God is considered weak and labeled as a high-risk for the Kingdom of Darkness. Therefore, he will be dealt with in the most brutal manner possible by his superiors, as the Kingdom of Darkness must take an unwelcomed loss due to his negligence.

It is also important to mention that not every spiritual entity that is detected by the gift of discernment will be evil in nature. There are times you will detect the Angels of God with you and it will feel nothing like the presence of evil. You will feel peace and sense their presence near you. Other times, you will detect kindred spirits of other believers. Your spirit will have a connection with them, since you are both in the same spiritual family (household of God) and residents of the same Kingdom (Kingdom of God). As such, you will be able to enjoy good fellowship with these people because you have shared interests in God. So, the gift of discernment is beneficial and essential for those who desire to be as useful to God as possible.

Faith

The gift of faith is one of the most powerful capabilities that prophets can possess because through faith, great and miraculous accomplishments materialize that are able to advance the Kingdom of God in the earthly realm. In fact, the book of Hebrews details many of the mighty achievements that occurred as a result of this supernatural gift being exerted by believers.

"By faith Abel offered unto God a more excellent sacrifice than Cain, by which he obtained witness that he was righteous, God testifying of his gifts: and by it he being dead yet speaketh. By faith Enoch was translated that he should not see death; and was not found, because God translated him: for before his translation he had this testimony, that he pleased God..." (Hebrews 11:4-38).

Yes, the bible is replete with great men and women of God who experienced scores of victories as they triumphed over much adversity. However, they were not considered great just because they were saved men and women in the bible. No, they were great because of the supernatural faith and confidence that each had demonstrated in their God's abilities. This upgraded faith made them courageous, unshakeable, and unstoppable. Such human vessels were ideal for a more heightened and expansive flow of God's unhindered power functioning through them. Moreover, the endowment of this faith can never be defined as ordinary faith attributed to average believers, as we have each been given a certain measure or capacity of faith for salvation and the necessary proportion of faith to accomplish the work God has appointed to us. But the gift of faith being the subject at hand happens to be a supernatural capability that God gives to specific people who must accomplish the impossible at pivotal moments in time. It is in these moments that God's sovereignty and ever abiding kingship is made known to both the earthly and celestial inhabitants. In case any person or creature in heaven or earth finds themselves challenging or pondering the validity of God's capabilities or credentials, the supercharged acts performed by prophets when operating in the gift of faith will eradicate all doubt.

"To the intent that now unto the principalities and powers in heavenly places might be known by the church the manifold wisdom of God, according to the eternal purpose which he purposed in Christ Jesus our Lord: In whom we have boldness and access with confidence by the faith of him." (Ephesians 3:10-12)

For the sake of time, we have discussed some of the gifts that prophets of God operate in just to give you an understanding of how important it is for these officers to hone and master their spiritual gifts. Every utilized gift gives us an advantage over our adversaries and positions us for victory, so we must be willing to avail ourselves of the spiritual gifts afforded to us in Christ.

"But the manifestation of the Spirit is given to every man to profit withal. For to one is given by the Spirit the word of wisdom; to another the word of knowledge by the same Spirit; To another faith by the same Spirit; to another the gifts of healing by the same Spirit; To another the working of miracles; to another prophecy; to another discerning of spirits; to another divers kinds of tongues; to another the interpretation of tongues: But all these worketh that one and the selfsame Spirit, dividing to every man severally as he will." (I Corinthians 12:7-11)

Cynthia Alvarez

CHAPTER 5
Prophets and The Law

Law Enforcement

In Chapter Four we focused on some of the spiritual gifts that are essential to the work of prophets. There is no possible way for these officers to meet the intense demands of their official duties without being skillful in the operation of spiritual gifts. Not only do they need to be capable of utilizing the gifts of the Spirit, but they must be well versed in the laws of God. Prophets are the law enforcement officers in the Kingdom. They make sure that God's laws are clearly understood, properly obeyed, and strictly enforced in the Kingdom of God on earth. But what laws of God are we speaking about? The laws that prophets are duty bound to address and enforce are all encompassed in the Ten Commandments of God. As it concerns these laws, prophets only see black or white; obedience or disobedience; righteousness or sin. They never see grounds or room for compromising the laws of God. For prophets, there is no such thing as a gray area that allows the ordinances of God to be averted by his people. This is clearly seen in his dealings with the nation of Israel in the bible. Whenever God had to chastise the nation of Israel it was because the people failed to keep His laws, which justified the harsh repercussions dealt to them. Furthermore, to ensure that Israel thoroughly understood the severity of their transgressions, prophets were always sent to speak his warnings, admonishments, and judgments to the nation. Likewise, when Israel honored God through continued obedience to his laws, prophets were sent to bless, restore, and edify them as his nation. God will not condone disobedience on any level, even Jesus, the only begotten son of the Father had to walk in obedience to the law of God during his 33 years of life on earth. In fact, Jesus was the only person capable of fulfilling the entire law of God without touching sin, but because he was sent to earth on a special mission by his father to redeem mankind, Jesus took upon him the sin of all humanity knowing that it would cost his life.

"And being found in fashion as a man, he humbled himself, and became obedient unto death, even the death of the cross." (Philippians 2:8)

So, we can clearly see God's purpose in raising up prophets in every generation who will ensure that his laws are always established, amplified, and strictly adhered to by his people.

God's Law – Ten Commandments (Exodus 20:2-17)
*How Prophets See His Law -Ten Commandments

1.   Thou shalt have no other gods before me. There is only one sovereign and eternal God, which means he has an absolute zero tolerance for any person, place or thing becoming a rival or contender to him in our lives. God will unquestionably never share his sovereignty with anyone for any reason whatsoever. For this reason, the flesh nature, the world, and Satan prove to be incessant rivals to the Lord God, as they contend with him for the right of way in besieging the souls of mankind. Seeing that such rivals of the Lord God exist, the people of God are to resist every attempt of his archrivals from infiltrating their lives to become the ruling fascism over them. If not, these rivals will emphatically become the lords, which rule over his people. To be overcome by such ruthless adversaries means one has failed or become negligent in keeping the first and most vital commandment of God. Therefore, the work of his prophets becomes necessary as they must enforce God laws by exposing the sin, announcing His judgment, and demonstrating his power against such atrocity.

2. Thou shalt not make unto thee any graven image, or any likeness of anything that is in heaven above, or that is in the earth beneath, or that is in the water under the earth. Thou shalt not bow down thyself to them, nor serve them: for I the Lord thy God am a jealous God, visiting the iniquity of the fathers upon the children unto the third and fourth generation of them that hate me; And shewing mercy unto thousands of them that love me, and keep my commandments. For man to create an image with the work of his own hands, ascribe it as being his god, and to worship it as God is blatant and open sin. It is a despicable abomination before God. To think that the creature could create a god in his own twisted imagination and reverence it as God is vile indeed. It would mean that the creature has become greater than his God, seeing that he is able to form what he perceives as God and worship him however he pleases, with little to no regard for who God is. But if man creates the Almighty and Eternal God in his own image through the works of his hands, that would make man the alpha and omega. It would make God a little lower than humanity. To view and reverence God any less than the Supreme Creator of heaven and earth would be to minimize his sovereignty, holiness, and eternality. It would make man the sum-total of divine perfection, which would make truth, righteousness, and holiness imperfect because without God, man can never even scratch the surface of perfection. Whenever mortal man resolves to crafting graven images as representations of his outlook on God, it results in idol gods being exalted, while the Almighty God is debased, discarded, and forbidden access into their hearts. In such degenerate conditions, the work of prophets becomes imperative and irrefutable.

3. **Thou shalt not take the name of the Lord thy God in vain; for the Lord will not hold him guiltless that taketh his name in vain.** Most believers think this commandment simply means not to use the Lord's name in a frivolous and playful fashion. It certainly is true, but this commandment spans much further than just frivolous play. It also applies to those professing Christians who love to name his name as being the Lord of their lives, but they are living hypocritical lifestyles filled with all manner of sin and ungodliness. Such degrading lifestyles only

promote the work of the enemy by giving him unsolicited opportunities to blaspheme God based on their unfruitful walk. When people are hypocrites and make claims about their intimacy, favor, and relationship with the Lord, they are using his name illegally, as they have no right to mention him in such cases that associate him with their ungodliness. God is not desperately seeking intimacy with hypocrites that put him at risk of intermingling with sin in any shape, form, or fashion. He does not negotiate with sin, as he has already judged sin. The word of God makes it clear that the soul that sins shall die. God is holy with or without man's approval. He is holy with or without man's ideologies and graven images. In fact, the Lord is holy with or without man's existence. So once again, the work of his prophets becomes necessary for such a time as this.

4. Remember the sabbath day, to keep it holy. Six days shalt thou labor, and do all thy work: But the seventh day is the sabbath of the Lord thy God: in it thou shalt not do any work, thou, nor thy son, nor thy daughter, thy manservant, nor thy maidservant, nor thy cattle, nor thy stranger that is within thy gates: For in six days the Lord made heaven and earth, the sea, and all that in them is, and rested the seventh day: wherefore the Lord blessed the sabbath day, and hallowed it. In the Old Testament, the nation of Israel was commanded to remember the Sabbath day and keep it holy, as it was a sign of their covenant with God. Therefore, they were to cease from their labor and toil on the seventh day of the week to devote themselves holy unto the Lord. It was a day for them to be set apart unto the Lord God, since they were unable to do such a thing while being slaves in Egypt. Being able to devote themselves to God on the Sabbath meant they honored the covenant made between them and God in an open way. Acknowledging this covenant on the seventh day was a crucial part of their lifestyle. It was an open display of allegiance and adherence to their God and his laws, which is what set them apart from all other nations who served false gods. No other nation was required to rest on the sabbath and keep it holy. False gods would never demand those who served them to be set apart to live a holy life for one second, let alone every seventh day. Satan would never tear down his own Kingdom with such contrary actions. In fact, his servants must sin every day of the week for as long as they live, if he is to be magnified in their lives; God requires holiness. It is no different for those of us who have entered in a New Covenant with Him. This covenant is so much better than the Old Covenant, since His Spirit indwells believers and causes every day to be the Sabbath for us. We do not have to wait until the seventh day of the week to devote ourselves to Him in reverence and fellowship. Now we can live a lifestyle of holiness every day and be set apart from sinners and unbelievers who would rather serve false gods that hold them in bondage to sin. We are free to keep covenant with God and enter into His presence for ourselves, if we continue abiding in Him while He abides in us. Yet, when believers break covenant with him through sin and transgression of the law, God must deal with the matter immediately in order to contain sin and prevent it from disseminating throughout the Body of Christ. Therefore, the work of His prophets comes to the forefront, as the will of God must be executed accordingly as it regards sin. God does not tolerate sin nor does his officers. Be not deceived.

5. Honor thy father and thy mother: that thy days may be long upon the land which the Lord thy God giveth thee. When one does not honor their father and mother, they essentially do not honor God. A child who does not honor his/her parents despises authority. If he/she despises authority, they despise God because all authority and power belongs to Him. Parents have been delegated by God to carry out the work of establishing, building, edifying, and securing the well-being of the family. Anything and anyone who opposes their father and mother, opposes God's purpose for the family. If God's purpose is opposed, it is considered an act of sin and the work of the prophets becomes necessary in such circumstances.

6. Thou shalt not kill. Let's be clear, the command is speaking to God's people about his law for them. God's people are not to kill one another as though they are enemies of God. The nation of Israel was instructed by God to destroy his enemies that withstood the Almighty and his people. Not only were they to destroy them, but their wives and children were also to be destroyed, so there would be no rudiments of these nations left to rise in power and withstand Israel again. It is no different for the people of God in this present age. He does not want Christians killing one another physically, emotionally, or mentally. Neither should Christians try to destroy one another financially in legal matters as the world does. They should be able to settle all matters of concern within the Body of Christ through the fivefold offices that God has established and empowered in every generation to carry out the work of teaching, correcting, reproving, and edifying believers. As it was physically required of the nation of Israel, so it is also spiritually required of Christians today to destroy the enemies of God, which are the flesh nature, the world, and Satan. Each of these enemies are required to be destroyed and killed off in the spiritual realm by believers. If there are believers who are not willing to kill off the enemies of God for their own selfish gain, the Body of Christ is to disassociate themselves from such individuals and give way for the necessary work of the prophets to be carried out on behalf of the Lord.

    7. **Thou shalt not commit adultery**. God requires fidelity in covenant relationships. He requires it of husbands and wives. He requires it first and foremost from those in the Body of Christ who are being prepared to be the Bride of Christ. Any woman who has a husband should never give her thoughts, heart, and her body to another man because it would violate the marriage covenant between the two; she is to be one with her husband. They are to be like-minded, have shared interests, exude the same affections towards one another, and be joined together intimately in body. If any area of this covenant is negatively affected by either the wife or the husband, the covenant becomes broken and instead of being one, they become divided. No longer do they think alike. Their affections have changed for one another, and the intimacy has been broken. The marriage has been breached by an outsider of the covenant. This is the same thing that happens when Christians refuse to be faithful to the Lord God. The most precious, intimate, and holiest relationship becomes breached by an outsider that is not even a partaker of the covenant. Once the covenant has been breached, the relationship is dismantled, and the work of the prophets becomes necessary.

    8. **Thou shalt not steal.** We all know that taking what does not belong to us is stealing. But withholding what belongs to someone else just because they are not aware that it belongs to them is thievery too. Anyone who purposely withholds the possessions of another just to make the person dependent upon them is a thief. People who take credit for the work and labor of someone else solely for their own financial gain are blatant thieves. Those who spend their lives scheming to find clever ways of swindling others out of their possessions are not just thieves, but they are calculating, conniving, and ruthless criminals. Furthermore, there are many in the Body of Christ who are guilty of such actions. Selfish-leaders who purposely mishandle God's truth to promote their own agenda within the Body of Christ just to be perceived as some great wonder by believers are nothing more than bonafide thieves. Withholding truth, wisdom, and knowledge keeps believers in an immature state, which does little to promote the purpose of God for them. God is expecting a harvest of mature believers that they might be established and positioned in His Kingdom. But to deny them truth, wisdom, and knowledge of God, is to rob him of the harvest that is rightfully his possession, as these leaders are stealing that which belongs to him. They are taking God's harvest for themselves. No question about it, the work of the prophets becomes necessary in such conditions.

9. Thou shalt not bear false witness against thy neighbor. Lying devastates individuals, families, cities, nations, countries, and has the capacity to affect the Body of Christ when believers exercise and accept it. To bear false witness is to twist the truth for self- satisfaction. A person who bears false witness has something to gain in doing so or else there would be no need to propagate a lie. When it comes to propagating a lie among believers, the motive is to deceive and stagnate growth within the Body of Christ. If believers are deceived, they lose sight of the Lord, His Kingdom, and his purpose for them. If growth is stagnated, believers will never reach their full potential in God and fall short of reaching destiny. Bearing false witness creates rippling effects within the Body of Christ because it affects relationships to the extent of dividing families, dissolving ministries, and breaking fellowship with God; with such apparent ramifications looming, the work of the prophets becomes exceedingly necessary.

10. Thou shalt not covet thy neighbor's house, thou shalt not covet thy neighbor's wife, nor his manservant, nor his maidservant, nor his ox, nor his ass, nor any thing that is thy neighbor's. It is true that God gives us what we do not deserve through grace. We did not earn it, deserve it, or expect it. He gave it to us freely through his love and kindness. However, when our outlook of life expresses the idea that whatever looks good, sounds goods, or feels good should become our possession, even if it rightfully belongs to someone else, it violates God's law. What makes it even more disturbing is that the ones we covet are not always distant, unknown, or hidden from us. But they are those closest to us who we see on a regular basis. Perhaps these would be people we fellowship and commune with, as the scripture uses the term neighbor, which signifies a closeness in proximity. It would have to be those who are close enough for us to get a glimpse of their possessions or holdings. How else could we be moved to covet what they have and provoked to take it for ourselves, if we were not in near proximity to them? So, it means that for the believers, our neighbors would be fellow Christians within the Body of Christ. If believers are covetous of one another, the Body of Christ is not functioning as one body, with one Spirit, and having one Lord but each person would be functioning independent of Christ, which impedes the purpose of the Lord for the Body of Christ. We all know that when the purpose of the Lord is frustrated, the work of the prophets becomes necessary, not optional.

CHAPTER 6
Prophets and Apostles
The Dream Team

In the previous chapters we discussed various aspects of prophets and found them to be mighty officers of God. While they are in a class all by themselves, prophets are also great Kingdom team players, especially when joining forces with apostles. Although the work of both prophets and apostles can be described as pivotal and powerful in every aspect, there is still nothing more awe inspiring than to see these two mighty offers working as a team to accomplish the will of God for His Kingdom on earth. As chief officers of the Lord, they are instrumental in breaking ground for the Kingdom, which means they are given the responsibility of impacting territories and lives that are resistant to the Lord and His Kingdom, as many people want nothing to do with Jesus or His Government. Yet, these mighty officers not only break ground, but they are also the Kingdom's defense system. They spiritually shield or protect the Kingdom of God on earth in similar manner as the ozone layer shields the natural inhabitants of earth from ultraviolet radiation. If the ozone layer is severely penetrated so that dangerous ultraviolet radiation successfully passes through this sphere or barrier of protection, many lives would be placed in harm's way because the atmosphere would become altered from its original state. When breached, the defense system is unable to safeguard the earth from imminent danger. In fact, the earth would be powerless against the effects of the ultraviolet rays that would invade it. Every creature on the planet would be susceptible to the effects of the radiation. Many people would be severely impacted on contact from the lethal rays while some would be moderately affected, if they took some measure of precaution by utilizing proper skincare treatments. Others who took evasive action in using proper skincare treatments and abiding in a place of shelter to avoid the ultraviolet rays would feel minimal effects of the radiation in their lives. In like manner, so it is with prophets and apostles. If intruders or contamination of any degree gains entrance into the Body of Christ, it would cause devastating effects in the Kingdom. Those who are weak in faith, would be severely impacted. Those who have some measure of validity in faith would be moderately affected while others who are stronger in faith would gradually become impacted by the breaches in the Kingdom. For this reason, these two chief officers must endure rigorous trials and encounter obstacles of unscaled magnitude to prepare them for the momentous work at hand. God must produce specific qualities within them to make them suitable Kingdom groundbreakers and certified defensive barriers. Without question, these officers must possess an extensive degree of **resolve**, **resilience**, and **reliability** if they are to properly safeguard the Kingdom. Nothing less will do, seeing that so much is at stake.

Resolve

No matter how intelligent, articulate, eager, popular or approachable any individual might be, if they do not possess the resolve that the Lord deems necessary to be a groundbreaker and defensive barrier for His Kingdom, He will never remotely consider them as possible candidates for either of these offices. Resolve is a non-negotiable qualification that prophets and apostles must possess, since they endure recurring high-level demonic assaults, setbacks, losses, disappointments, and betrayals.

"And Jesus said unto him, no man, having put his hand to the plough, and looking back, is fit for the kingdom of God." (Luke 9:62)

Without having a substantial measure of resolve, an individual would be ineffective in fulfilling the duties of God's officials. It would be impossible for them to withstand the strength of the adversaries of the Kingdom because their commitment to God and their official post would become easily compromised, as they would not be willing to endure the stress, brutality, and eventualities of such demanding offices. Unfortunately, resolve is something that simply cannot be overlooked when it comes to God appointing his officials.

Resilience

Prophets and apostles are officers of the highest caliber in the Kingdom. They have a valuable Kingdom outlook that is central to the execution of their overall duties. For them, the King and His Kingdom are first and foremost in their lives, in fact, it is what fuels their passionate drive to see that the Kingdom is manifested on earth, even if it costs their lives. Having such an inner driving force enables them to bounce back or recover quickly from traumatic events in their lives that would easily take out the average believer. Whether it is physical illness, death of a loved one, loss of a job, or ostracization, these officers are not shaken to the point of abandoning their office. They continue to perform as proficiently as God requires of them.

"Yea doubtless, and I count all things but loss for the excellency of the knowledge of Christ Jesus my Lord: for whom I have suffered the loss of all things, and do count them but dung, that I may win Christ." (Philippian 3:8)

It is resilience that allows prophets and apostles to rise above adversity and continue to move forward in the Kingdom agenda of God. Without having the grit or resilience to make a quick comeback from any challenge or difficulty, the Kingdom would undoubtedly be overrun by the enemy. But God has appointed these mighty officers to break ground for the King and stand in the defense of the Kingdom to ensure that it is established and expanding according to his agenda. God does not make exceptions or retract his qualifications for these two officers. His standards are irrevocable concerning these Kingdom officials and he will not budge in the slightest detail, since the Kingdom is the overall subject at hand.

Reliability

Nothing is more pressing to God concerning prophets and apostles than their reliability. The extensive knowledge, dynamic gifts, and unfathomable revelations that have been entrusted to them by God means little to nothing, if he cannot depend on them being at his disposal.

"And when they had brought their ships to land, they forsook all, and followed him." (Luke 5:11)
So, to ensure that these officers always remain loyal to him, God will deal decisively and specifically with everything and everyone that has a tight grip on the heart of the prophets and apostles. Some of the relationships and connections to these officers will be terminated all together while other relationships will be revamped to fit within the specified guidelines that he has established in the lives of His Kingdom officers. Seeing that they spend most of their time in fellowship with God, it is only befitting that he takes great concern with who and what is connected to them. Why would he establish such powerful Kingdom offices, appoint chosen vessels to execute the duties of the offices, and send them forth into a foreign land that we know as this present evil world, yet not be

concerned with them being reliable officials? Reliability is of the utmost importance, since they have been heavily endowed with his authority and power. As God continues to raise up prophets and apostles for the work of establishing His Kingdom, reliability will always be an interwoven thread in these mantles.

    A unique and impressive quality of prophets and apostles is their ability to war effectively in the Spirit through decrees and fervent prayers. God has groomed these mighty officers to be fearless in the Spirit and a force to be reckoned with in battle. This can be clearly seen when they speak forth powerful decrees and amplified prayers, since these officers have phenomenal leverage in the spiritual realm and understand how to reach or hit the correct level or frequency needed to summon the angelic brigades of God. I know some people might not feel that it is a big deal that these officers can summon angelic assistance when necessary. But they do more than just speak forth a whisper to summon these angels. Prophets and apostles speak with Kingdom authority and fervency because they summon angels from different levels and various spheres of the spiritual realm. So, it takes a specific pitch, special frequency, and certain grade of authority to cause God's mighty angelic army to heed the charge of men. Soft and timid spoken decrees will not muster the angelic forces needed to engage an army of darkness because it cannot yield the appropriate pitch or emit the proper signal needed to arouse God's celestial warriors. Nor will lukewarm and apathetic prayer bring about change on any level (spiritual or physical). Again, there is a certain pitch and frequency needed. In fact, with prayer, there is a certain temperature required. Prayer needs to reach a boiling point because it must ascend to a higher realm. It is no different than when water boils and turns into vapor. Only when the water vaporizes or transforms into a different form does it move higher into the atmosphere. Prayer is not meant to remain in the lower depths of the physical realm. But it is meant to ascend to the spiritual realm and impact that sphere to cause metamorphosis to take place in the earthly realm. Yes, decrees and prayers released from the mouths of prophets and apostles of God become weapons of mass destruction and mighty tools of Kingdom advancement. It stands to reason that He has meticulously crafted the anointing necessary to enable these two officers to strategically and fearlessly stand in the gate of two realms and brandish immense power and authority to establish the Kingdom of God on earth.

"The effectual fervent prayer of a righteous man availeth much. Elias was a man subject to like passions as we are, and he prayed earnestly that it might not rain: and it rained not on the earth by the space of three years and six months. And he prayed again, and the heaven gave rain, and the earth brought forth her fruit." (James 5:16-18)

There is no questioning the weight of the workload of God's officers in this hour. Many people might see them as stringent and intransigent, as they refuse to deviate from the all-encompassing will of God. Prophets and apostles are well versed in what they have been called to do for God. They are not ignorant to the impact they have on the Body of Christ, since much of what they do is geared towards keeping believers connected to the Person of God and not just making sure they are acquainted with his power. It is not enough that believers experience the power of God only, but they must form a genuine and intimate relationship with him to have dominion in the Kingdom. So, these officers lead believers into dominion by helping them forge a solid relationship with God above all else. Knowing that Satan is relentless in opposing or counteracting the formation of such a relationship between believers and God, these officers must remain staunch and stringent in the work of the Kingdom. If they falter at all in establishing believers in Christ and safeguarding the Kingdom, dominion would be beyond the scope of achievement for believers. Yet, the strength of prophets and apostles lies within their private and personal relationship with God. There is nothing quite like the bond between God and his chief officials. This relationship situates them as family, friends, and employees of the Almighty God; therefore, they encounter a broader scope of interactions with him that go far beyond what most believers experience. All believers are included in God's family or household because they are in Christ, but all believers are not considered to be his closest friends, as this level of relationship demands more from them. Being in friendship with God means that believers must grow in his knowledge and grace, since being friends means you both share interests and goals of some sort.

"Henceforth I call you not servants; for the servant knoweth not what his lord doeth: but I have called you friends; for all things that I have heard of my Father I have made known unto you." (John 15:14-15)

Yet, many believers show very little growth in his knowledge and grace, which means they simply cannot interact with him on a level of genuine friendship. However, being employed by God means that you are not only considered to be his family and friends, but you are trustworthy enough to handle Kingdom administration. Believers must clearly understand that for believers, God is the fullness of everything they will ever need. He is Lord, Savior, King, Father, Lawyer, Doctor, Provider, Protector, and much more because he has the credentials to support these claims. Furthermore, he also grooms his officers to be a fully functioning support system to effectively undergird the workload and meet the needs of the Body of Christ.

"To the weak became I as weak, that I might gain the weak: I am made all things to all men, that I might by all means save some. And this I do for the gospel's sake, that I might be partaker thereof with you." (I Corinthians 9:22-23)

Therefore, when speaking of prophets and apostles, it is evident that God regards them as useful and beneficial to Kingdom administration. This is not to insinuate that they are loved by God more than any other believer, since God loves all believers with the same love. It is simply to give readers and idea of certain aspects of the work performed by these officers while keeping in mind that God chooses his officials and he will always do what is in the best interest of the Kingdom.

ABOUT THE AUTHOR

Cynthia Alvarez is a dedicated servant of the Lord Jesus Christ. Her passion for the King and his Kingdom is undeniable as she continues to empower the Body of Christ in this hour. The goal of her work is to break believers out of the typical church pattern by acclimating them to the culture of the Kingdom of God. *'Apostles'* is nothing less than remarkable and life altering in every way. It is one of several books written by Cynthia Alvarez that is designed to transform lives and produce a harvest of souls that are qualified for dominion in the Kingdom of our eternal Lord and Savior Jesus Christ.

A special thanks to all who have supported the endeavors of Cynthia Alvarez with your purchase of this book. May the blessings of our Lord Jesus Christ richly increase you above measure.

Cynthia Alvarez

ABOUT THE BOOK

Prophets is a thought-provoking book that will challenge your view on God's mighty officer. It will arouse your hunger for not only the prophetic realm, but it will cause those who are prophets to respond to the call of God in this hour, as it confirms what has already been revealed to them. Many who are being called by God in this hour feel the prophetic fire within, but simply do not know what to do about it. Well, the time for you to find your place and walk in the fire of God's calling as a prophet is now. This book will transform your life by opening your eyes to see the broader scope of his prophets. You no longer need to feel like an outcast, as if no one understands you or your struggles. *Prophets* was written for people everywhere who know there is more that God has ordained for them to do in this life. They know that God has called them to change the world in their lifetime. Without question, you will be empowered to do so after reading this book.

Prophets

Cynthia Alvarez

Prophets

Cynthia Alvarez